+BF311 .W5947

AUDREY COHEN COLLEGE

50664000142390
Witkin, Herman A/Cognitive styles in per
BF311 .W5947 C.1 STACKS 1978

BF
311
W5947

Witkin, Herman A.
Cognitive styles
in personal and
cultural adaptation

DATE DUE

D1802300

COGNITIVE STYLES IN PERSONAL AND CULTURAL ADAPTATION

Drawing by Leonard Baskin

Cognitive Styles in Personal and Cultural Adaptation

by Herman A. Witkin

CLARK UNIVERSITY PRESS

1978

COLLEGE FOR HUMAN SERVICES
LIBRARY
345 HUDSON STREET
NEW YORK, N.Y. 10014

Copyright 1978 by Clark University Press.

Library of Congress Cataloging in Publication Data
Witkin, Herman A.
  Cognitive styles in personal and cultural adaptation.

  (Heinz Werner lecture series; 1977)
  Includes bibliographical references and index.
  1. Cognitive styles. 2. Personality. 3. Personality and culture. I. Title. II. Series: Heinz Werner lectures; 1977.
BF311.W5947   155.2'3   77-12426
ISBN 0-914206-10-9

The Heinz Werner Lectures

Ludwig von Bertalanffy
Organismic Psychology and Systems Theory, 1966.

Jean Piaget
On the Development of Memory and Identity, 1967.

Jerome S. Bruner
Processes of Cognitive Growth: Infancy, 1968.

Roman Jakobson
The Paths from Infancy to Language, 1969.

Conrad H. Waddington
Biology, Purpose and Ethics, 1970.

Kenneth Burke
Dramatism and Development, 1971.

Rene Dubos
Of Human Diversity, 1972.

Errol E. Harris
Perceptual Assurance and the Reality of the World, 1973.

Bernard Kaplan
Rationality and Irrationality in Development, 1974.

J. McVicker Hunt
Early Psychological Development and Experience, 1976.

Herman A. Witkin
Cognitive Styles in Personal and Cultural Adaptation, 1977.

The Heinz Werner Lecture Series

This is the eleventh of The Heinz Werner Lecture Series. This series is designed to provide a forum for outstanding scholars who are known for their contributions to the developmental analysis of biological, psychological and/or socio-cultural phenomena. This series is sponsored by the Heinz Werner Institute of Developmental Psychology.

Heinz Werner (1890-1964) was one of the leading psychologists of the past half century. Deeply impressed by processes of organic formation and ordered change in various domains of the life sciences, he sought to apply developmental conceptualization and developmental analysis to all aspects of existence in which mentality is manifested. Convinced that developmental psychology is not merely a subject matter but is, rather, a manner of conceptualizing all psychological phenomena, Werner sought to encompass animal behavior, ontogenesis, pathological phenomena, products of collective activity, and behavior evoked in experimental situations, within a comprehensive system—a general psychology, grounded in the fundamental concept of development. In accord with Werner's philosophy, the Heinz Werner Institute of Developmental Psychology is devoted to the application of developmental analysis to all psycho-biological and psycho-cultural phenomena. It seeks to fulfill Werner's vision by promoting research and teaching at graduate and post-graduate levels which will serve to integrate the various life sciences without collapsing their distinctiveness in method and subject matter.

Bernard Kaplan Clark University
Seymour Wapner

Contents

INTRODUCTION 1

ONE/THE NATURE OF COGNITIVE STYLES 6
  Field Dependence-Independence and Psychological Differentiation 15

TWO/COGNITIVE STYLES IN HUMAN ADAPTATION 30
  Attunement of Cognitive Styles to Life Situations 30
  Choice of Life Situations Adaptive to Cognitive Styles 42
  Development of Behaviors Adaptive to Cognitive Styles 50
  Adaptation to the Cognitive Style of Another 56
  Mobility and Fixity in the Use of Cognitive Styles 58

THREE/INDIVIDUALITY AND DIVERSITY 62

REFERENCES 67

Introduction*

Because of my personal and intellectual ties to the man whose work and memory we are honoring, my participation in this lecture series has very special meaning for me. Heinz Werner was a good and valued friend and his theoretical system has had an important influence on my own life's work. In our use of his concepts and of the developmental approach he espoused, the research my colleagues and I have done over the years bears an obvious debt to Werner. I trust that our work, in turn, has made some contribution to Werner's developmental conception. There are two main ways in which I think we have done so, still in Werner's lifetime. One was by extending the concept of differentiation to include domains commonly subsumed under personality. The other was by concerning ourselves with individuality as expressed in cognitive styles. Late in his career, Werner emphasized the need for greater attention to individuality in developmental theory. "The conviction has been growing in recent years," he wrote, "that developmental conceptualization, in order to reaffirm its truly organismic character, has to expand its orbit of interest to include as an actual problem the study of individuality" (Werner, 1957, p. 146). That Werner looked favorably on our efforts is suggested by what he wrote in the Foreword to our book, *Psychological Differentiation*, in 1962.

Since then, as I will tell you in these talks, we have gone even farther afield by attempting to encompass within the framework of differentiation theory the domains of interpersonal behavior, neurophysiological functioning and modes of individual and cultural adap-

*The preparation of these lectures was aided by a grant (MH 21989) from the National Institute of Mental Health.

tation. I would like to believe that Werner would also have found these departures congenial to his theoretical perspective.

The task my title sets for me is to consider the role of cognitive styles in personal and cultural adaptation. Before undertaking that task, however, I need to give my current conception of what I believe cognitive styles to be. This is necessary because it is in the more recent developments that we find the most compelling theoretical grounds for linking cognitive styles to adaptation and the most impressive evidence of such a linkage.

That cognitive styles have the potential of serving adaptive ends was an idea implicit in the very earliest conception of them. This idea was also fostered by the Zeitgeist which first stimulated interest in them. Work on cognitive styles began to appear in the late 1940s—although not then called by that name—as part of a loose confederation of research efforts. These efforts were a response to the inadequacies many of us felt existed in the traditional approaches to perception then in vogue. However different their particular discontents and their proposed remedies, the representatives of these efforts joined forces in claiming that the traditional approaches had not made adequate room for the perceiver in perception. The movement acquired a name, "The New Look," which helped give it a public identity. The double entendre of the name, when applied to perception, made it very catchy. As a small footnote to history, it is worth mentioning that the name was actually taken from the popular designation for the long full-skirted dress style Christian Dior had made fashionable at about that time.

The claim made by the New Look psychologists on behalf of the perceiver was, of course, not being voiced for the first time in the history of psychology. We need only recall Wilhelm Stern's earlier famous dictum, directed against Gestalt theory: "Keine Gestalt ohne Gestalter." It is commonplace in the growth of any science for what appears to be the same issue to arise over and over again. Perhaps reflecting Werner's principles of spirality, however, the issue and its treatment are likely to take different forms at different times, mirroring the developmental stage of the science at the moment. So it is that the questions asked and the answers proposed in the late forties on the perceiver's place in perception were unique to the prevailing conceptual context.

The diversity of the proposals intended to give the perceiver his due, and the vigor of the research done to test these proposals, made the late forties and early fifties an enormously exciting time to be working in perception. The New Look went public in 1949 at an APA symposium (chaired by Heinz Werner in fact) entitled "Personal and Social Factors in Perception." A collection of the symposium papers, and additional papers by other investigators working in the same idiom, appeared the following year in a book, *Perception and Personality* (Bruner and Krech, 1950). Among the papers, we find represented most of the psychologists who gave the New Look movement its early impetus, and most of the conceptions and research approaches involved in the movement. One group of studies reported in the volume examined the influence of a wide array of organismic attributes—values, needs, attitudes, tonic states—on perceptual functioning. Another group of studies was concerned with the interrelated phenomena of perceptual defense and subliminal perception. Still another group considered the nature and bases of individual differences in perceiving, the stuff out of which cognitive styles came to be made.

The 1949 symposium, and the volume which emerged from it, symbolized for many the great potential of the New Look approach. The product of that optimism was an outpouring of research and theory, recorded in a very large literature. I will not attempt to evaluate the overall impact of that effort, viewed from the vantage point of the present. Because the New Look movement was a loose confederation, the fate of its components has varied considerably. Whatever the fate of the other components, the cognitive-style component remains an active field of inquiry more than two-and-a-half decades later; in fact, it has extended its reach into many domains of psychology outside of perception, where it started, and into adjacent disciplines as well.

Since 1949, research on cognitive styles has been carried on in many research centers, leading to the identification of a number of cognitive styles. Familiar in the psychological vernacular by now are such stylistic dimensions as leveling-sharpening, constricted-flexible control, strong vs. weak automatization, scanning, field dependence-independence, conceptualizing, reflection-impulsivity, to mention the main ones. Although the cognitive styles on record are numerous, they differ considerably among themselves in their development of theoretical rationale, extent of empirical underpinning, availability of adequate assessment procedures, amount of information about their origins and their ramifications in personal functioning, and evidence of their implications for everyday life. I think it not unfair to say that, on most of these counts, field dependence-independence is farthest along among members of the family of cognitive styles. Included in the large literature now on record are studies of field dependence-independence in areas as diverse as interpersonal behavior, learning and memory, perceptual constancies, defense mechanisms, autonomic nervous system processes, cultural differences, dreaming, schizophrenia, child-rearing, laterality, and moral judgment. That literature shows as well that field dependence-independence has found application to practical issues as diverse as academic and occupational choices, alcohol addiction, driving safety, progress of patients in psychotherapy, reading difficulty, and teacher behavior. The reasons for the disproportionate research investment in the field-dependent and field-independent cognitive styles over others lie, I believe, in the start of research on these styles in extensive laboratory studies of perception, in their salience and pervasiveness in the individual's psychological functioning, in their placement in a broad conceptual framework, and in their demonstrated representation in many important real-life settings.

ONE

The Nature of Cognitive Styles

The developed theoretical base and extensive empirical underpinning of the field-dependent and field-independent cognitive styles make them particularly good exemplars to use in forming a conception of what cognitive styles are like. I will now examine these styles with that purpose in mind. The conception we will come out with carries, in my view, the essential qualifications which dimensions must meet to merit the designation "cognitive style," however diverse they may be in other particulars. I shall consider the concept of cognitive styles in some detail out of a belief that clarity about their essential nature is important for understanding their role in adaptation. Because in talking about cognitive styles I will be identifying their potential for entering into the service of adaptation, by the time we come to consider adaptation directly we will be halfway home on that issue.

A sense of what the field-dependent and field-independent cognitive styles are all about might best be conveyed by an historic account of the development of research on these styles, and of the theory that evolved to accommodate the results of that research. There is hardly time to tell here a story that has taken three decades to unfold. While I must limit myself mainly to the conception as it now stands, I think it will be useful to take a little time for that part of the very early history which first brought individual diversity to attention. That, after all, is how it started. In particular, I want to describe some phenomena incidentally observed during work then in progress. These observations generated hunches and intuitions of the kind that never get written down in published papers, though powerful motive forces in research. The phenomena were so dramatic, and seemed so clearly to connect with the heart of the psyche that, as I describe them, you may see why I soon felt compelled to pursue them in their own right. You may also be able to see how it has been possible for their pursuit to generate enough work to occupy me and many other investigators for some decades now; and the job of understanding these phenomena is far from done.

The studies I draw upon for the observations I want to bring to your attention were undertaken as a challenge to Ernst Mach's classical egocentric theory of space orientation. That challenge was launched from the perspective of field theory, a position I espoused as a devoted Gestalt psychologist. In fact, these studies were carried out under a fellowship I held, sponsored by the veritable fountainheads of Gestalt psychology: Max Wertheimer and, after Wertheimer's death, Wolfgang Kohler. The studies were concerned with perception of the upright. In the experimental paradigm these studies employed, subjects' judgments of the upright were obtained after separating the visual and bodily standards— in other words, the field and egocentric standards— ordinarily used in determining the upright. These standards commonly coincide in direction; each accordingly leads to precisely the same location of the upright. By separating them, the location of the upright is likely to be different, depending upon which standard is followed.

It is now ancient history that, in one situation we used, the separation of the two standards was accomplished by having the erect subject view a tilted luminous frame in a totally darkened room, with the request that he adjust to the upright a tilted luminous rod centered within the tilted frame.[1] In a second situation, the subject was seated in a chair within a tilted room, and his task now was to adjust his own body to the upright. In both situations, separation of the visual and bodily standards was accomplished by displacing the axes of the visual field while leaving the force on the body unchanged. In a third situation, the separation was accomplished in an opposite manner. The subject was seated in a small, lighted, fully-enclosed, upright room which was driven around a circular track. This motion created a force on the body which was the resultant between the downward pull of gravity and the centrifugal force generated by the rotation. Here then, it was the direction of the force on the body that was changed while the visual field remained upright. Experiments with these three situations contributed to a better understanding of the processes underlying orientation to the upright, and to some enlightenment on the theoretical issue of egocentrism vs. field factors in space orientation, for which the experiments were initially undertaken.

I bypass these matters and turn to some of the observations made in the course of these experiments which bear on the individual-diversity issue. One observation, unexpected and baffling to me as a rather orthodox Gestalt psychologist, was that in all three orientation tasks people differed markedly in the extent to which they used the body or the visual field as referents for judging the upright. The same field factors—and for that matter, the same combination of field factors and bodily stimulation—did not guarantee the same perceptual outcome for all people. This suggested that the person contributes in an important way to the process of orientation toward the upright in space. Accordingly, that contribution must somehow be taken into account if a full understanding of the process is to be achieved.

[1] References for specific studies referred to in this monograph are not cited, although review papers and books are referenced. Comprehensive bibliographies on field dependence-independence and psychological differentiation are available elsewhere (Witkin, Oltman, Cox, Ehrlichman, Hamm, and Ringler, 1973; Witkin, Cox, Friedman, Hrishikesan, and Siegel, 1974; Witkin, Cox, and Friedman, 1976).

Another observation was that subjects showed impressive self-consistency, across situations and over long periods of time, in their degree of reliance on body or field in locating the upright. People thus seemed to have characteristic and enduring ways of processing information from body and visual field.

There were other observations which suggested that the person's preferred way of perceiving in these experimental situations was revealing something rather important about him. As one example, I noticed that some subjects, in adopting the axes of the visual field as a referent, did so at the expense of total suppression of strong sensations of body tilt. I recall one subject from the early days when the tilting-room, tilting-chair apparatus was still a brand new toy for me. When this subject was tilted 22° left, and the experimental room around him was tilted 35° left, he confidently reported that he was tilted to the *right*, and that in order for him to be straight he had to be moved to the *left*. I assumed at first that he was mixing up left and right, so I asked him to point to the direction in which he wanted to be moved. Unhesitatingly, he pointed to the left. When he had reached a tilt of 35° left, so that he was aligned with the room tilted at that same angle, he said he was now straight. He answered in the affirmative such questions as whether he was at that point sitting the way he ordinarily sat in class or when eating his dinner. To appreciate what was going on with this subject, try sometime to sit in a chair tipped over at a 35° angle. Then imagine, if you can, not feeling at all the strong sensations from your own body produced by being tipped over that far. Psychology's concern with the content of human experience makes its subject matter commonplace, so that new phenomena are a rarity. For me, the behavior of this subject—which I subsequently encountered in other subjects—was out of the realm of ordinary experience or even what seemed possible on the basis of ordinary experience. In fact, so novel did this behavior seem that I went out into the hallway to invite a passing colleague to observe it. What was of course involved in this subject's behavior was that he used the visual axes of the experimental room as an exclusive referent, and in relation to the axes of the room, tilted 35° to the left, he himself, tilted 22° left, was indeed to the right. It should be added that when this subject, after reporting himself to be straight while aligned with the room tilted at 35° left, was asked to close his eyes, he immediately experienced the full magnitude of his tilt. With eyes closed, he was able to bring himself to within about a degree or two of the upright. His behavior with the tilted room in view was thus a function of the visual-postural conflict to which he had been exposed, rather than the result of any sensory or neural defect.

Observations of what happened to some subjects when they encountered difficulty in reconciling their conflicting visual and postural experiences provided another indication that performance in the orientation tests caught the person at the quick. Sometimes a subject in the body-adjustment test, soon after opening his eyes at the beginning of a trial, when he and the experimental room were tilted and both stationary, said he was unable to tell his position in space, complained of feeling ill, and asked to be let out of the apparatus. Those who had encountered such a feeling in other circumstances had a name for it: an anxiety attack.

Still another set of observations showed that a person's preferred way of perceiving was highly compelling for him and not easily overcome. This again suggested that the diversity in individual performances I was becoming concerned with could hardly be trivial. To illustrate, let me describe a subject in the body-adjustment test who, like the subject I described earlier, reported himself to be straight when he was aligned with the tilted room. As part of a training program directed at changing his preferred way of perceiving, I handed him a plumb line. As happened with his body, so did it happen with the plumb line that, under the influence of the tilted room, the plumb line appeared to be tilted in the direction opposite to the tilt of the room. Objectively, it was hanging straight down of course. So real was the subject's impression of the plumb line being tilted that when I asked how a plumb line he was holding freely in his own hand could be other than straight, he proposed that I was directing a blast of air against it. When, at my invitation, he searched and found no air current, he decided that I had placed a magnet outside the room that was pulling the metal plumb to one side.

These strange phenomena were all observed in experimental situations. Take, for example, the phenomenon of a person who, when tilted 35°, with the room at the same angle of tilt, experienced himself as fully straight. Although observed under special circumstances, this occurrence inevitably provoked the question: What might it be saying about a person, in a more general way, that a host of compelling sensations from within his own body can go unfelt as he accedes to the influence of the surrounding visual field? Might this behavior reflect his typical manner of handling his impulses? Connections to personality thus suggested themselves quite early. Involvement of the body in the perceptual processes studied early on was important in other ways in suggesting that the observed diversity among individuals should be taken seriously. Because the body is the vehicle of the self, perceptual experiences in which the body is at issue are especially likely to be connected with psychological essences. Thus, it is understandable that uncertainty about one's own position could prove so disturbing as to make the person feel anxious and ill. One would hardly expect, nor have I ever encountered, such reactions from subjects when they were uncertain about the distance of an object or the pitch of a tone. It is also much more attention-getting to the experimenter to encounter a subject who is mistaken about the position of his body in space than a subject in error about the brightness of an object.

These, then, were among the side observations which made it apparent that people differ in how they process information from body and field in determining the upright, and that an adequate understanding of perception of the upright could not be achieved without putting the person's characteristic way of processing information into the formula, along with field factors and sensory experiences. Gertrude Stein, on first beholding Oakland, is reported to have said: "But there is no there out there." As the observations, hunches and intuitions I have been citing piled up, my reaction to the individual-diversity issue was, "there really is a there out there." The individual differences I had been noting could not be simply dismissed as so much random noise of a kitten on a keyboard. You can imagine that in determining to include the characteristics of the individual in the further study of space orientation, I was departing from Gestalt psychology, which hardly provides a cozy home for considering individual diversity. Let me stress that, for me, attention to individual diversity was not an end in itself. It was rather in the service of conceptualizing processes of space orientation and, later, processes of personal functioning and development.

It was important for the cognitive-style research pathway which subsequently emerged that the work on the field-dependent and field-independent cognitive styles had its beginnings in laboratory investigations of the perceptual processes which we now believe to be at the heart of these styles. That early laboratory work was a valuable source of knowledge for conceptualizing these styles. It was also the source of a methodology for assessing them. When the need later arose for assessment procedures to determine people's standing on the field-dependence-independence dimension, we were able to draw on that laboratory work in developing a battery of tests, providing multiple measures of the dimension.

Since those early days when individual diversity began to take its place in the conceptual and empirical development of our program of research, many colleagues have contributed their heads, hands, and hearts to its progress. My main collaborators in the program at different periods have been Solomon Asch, Ruth Dyk, Hanna Faterson, Donald Goodenough, Max Hertzman, Stephen Karp, Helen Lewis, Karen Machover, Pearl Meissner, Philip Oltman, and Seymour Wapner. Numerous other investigators at many different institutions, often following quite different approaches from our own, have contributed extensively to both knowledge and theory in the development of this line of endeavor.

As is typical of any long-range programmatic research, our work has been characterized over the years by continuous interplay between theory and evidence. As the evolving theory was put to empirical test at each stage of its development, the evidence derived from that testing was fed back into the theory to make its propositions more precise and its hypotheses more specific. The newly modified theory then served as a guide for the next empirical step, again with its built-in feedback loop; and so the process has continued. Our way of working has, I believe, followed the approach Werner advocated when he described the role of the investigator as "discoverer and explorer of unknown lands." He wrote that

> hypotheses . . . are essential elements of inquiry, but they are so . . . as flexible parts of the process of searching; by the same token, conclusions drawn from the results, again, are as much an end as a beginning; . . . looking back in the direction of the initial hypothesis (experimental findings) represent a momentary solution and, looking forward, they represent a problem, a hypothesis for further inquiry. . . . Research (is) essentially a problem-solving procedure, a probing into unknown territories with plans that are not readily fixed but modifiable, with progress and retreat, with branching out into various directions or concentration on one (Werner, 1962, pp. 4-5).

A major conceptual step we took, in 1962, was the formulation of the theory of psychological differentiation (Witkin, Dyk, Faterson, Goodenough, and Karp, 1962/1974). That theoretical statement sought, first of all, to accommodate the linkages established by then between individual diversity in perception of the upright and diversity in ways of functioning ordinarily considered parts of personality, such as controls and defenses, body concept, and sense of identity. The theory sought as well to place the individual patterns observed, now quite broad in scope, in a developmental framework. Very recently, we proposed a further revision and extension of differentiation theory to accommodate newly accumulated evidence on interpersonal behavior, cognitive restructuring skills, and neurophysiological specialization (Witkin and Goodenough, 1976). Compared to the earlier model of differentiation, the newly proposed one has a larger number of delineated constructs and a more hierarchical structure. In its conceptualization of the field-dependent and field-independent cognitive styles, it proposes some changes in our earlier usage of the concepts of "cognitive style" and "field dependence-independence." In brief, we have taken a new New Look at cognitive styles.

Our current statement of field-dependence theory, and its parent theory of psychological differentiation, is another way station on a theory-building journey which is still very much in progress. Because my focus here is on cognitive styles, and my time limited, I can do no more than touch lightly on aspects of differentiation theory beyond the parts in which field dependence-independence is directly implacated.

✿ ✿ ✿ ✿ ✿

Field Dependence-Independence and Psychological Differentiation

In briefest terms, differentiation refers to the complexity of structure of a psychological system. Particular formal arrangements, determined by a given degree of differentiation, influence the development of typical ways of functioning. Judgments about degree of differentiation can thus be made through specific functional manifestations. Greater differentiation manifests itself, first of all, in segregation of psychological activities within the organism. The separate, specialized functions resulting from segregation are interrelated into a hierarchical structure, and so are integral constituents of an articulated system. One instance of segregation of psychological functions is the development of controls over impulse expression and of specialized defenses for warding off potentially disturbing feelings. Another instance is the development of an articulated conception of the body. A second way in which differentiation shows itself is in self-nonself segregation. Boundaries are formed between the self and the outside world, of which other people are of course the most salient component. Because a given level of differentiation is conceived to be a characteristic of the organism as a whole, greater self-nonself segregation is likely to "go with" greater segregation of psychological functions, making for consistency in behavior. Further reflecting its organismic character, greater differentiation is also likely to show itself in the neurophysiological domain, again in the form of segregation of functions, contributing still further to consistency across domains.

I am going to focus on the self-nonself segregation aspect of differentiation because that is where field dependence-independence has its conceptual home. Development of a segregated self carries with it the formation of internal frames of reference. The availability of internal referents and the greater polarity between self and others, which self-nonself segregation implies, contribute to greater determination of behavior from within. On the other hand, the lesser repertoire of internal standards and the continued connection with others associated with limited self-nonself segregation are likely to encourage reference to external sources as guides to behavior. Greater or less self-nonself segregation is thus conceived as influencing the degree of emphasis placed on internal or external referents in processing information which has self and field as its source. The tendency to rely primarily on internal referents in a self-consistent way we designate a *field-independent* cognitive style. The tendency to give greater credit to external referents is a *field-dependent* cognitive style. It is, in part, because the one tendency or the other is a pervasive characteristic of the person that the designation "style" seems appropriate. The reason for designating these styles "field dependent" and "field independent" is self-evident. The contrasting tendencies represented in these styles, it seems reasonable to believe, find expression in the three orientation tests I described earlier, the rod-and-frame test, the body-adjustment test, and the rotating-room test. To the extent that scores from these tests form a continuous distribution, the labels field independent and field dependent represent tendencies, varying in degree of strength, to rely primarily on internal or external referents. Certainly, we are not dealing with two distinct categories of people.

While, as we saw, individuals are consistent in their tendency to place greater reliance on self or field as referents across the three orientation tests, one tendency does not necessarily make for more veridical perception than the other. As is typical of process variables, whether use of a field-dependent or field-independent mode leads to a more accurate outcome or not, depends on the immediate context. Take the rod-and-frame and body-adjustment tests. In both, the visual field is tilted and the direction of the force on the body corresponds to the true upright. Field-dependent people, by using the visual surround as a primary referent, end up far off the true upright in both situations, as we saw; field-independent people, by relying on the body, come out with a quite accurate determination. Now, in contrast, take the rotating-room test. Here, you will recall, the force on the body is displaced while the visual field remains upright. The very same tendency field-dependent people show in the rod-and-frame and body-adjustment tests to adhere to the axes of the prevailing visual field makes them highly accurate in the rotating-room test. Field-independent people, by continuing to follow their characteristic approach of relying primarily on the body, are now highly inaccurate.

The distinction between process and product, evident in these examples of the variety of achievements that may follow from use of a given cognitive style, is one that Heinz Werner constantly stressed.

The tendencies to rely primarily on internal or external referents in perception of the upright have been shown to express themselves, in congruent fashion, in the individual's social behavior. A large body of literature, recently reviewed by Witkin and Goodenough (1977), has shown that more field-independent people, who use their own bodies as a referent in perception of the upright, also function more autonomously of the social field than do field-dependent people.

The internal frames of reference available to field-independent people enable them to structure situations on their own. Field-dependent people, on the other hand, having less access to internal referents, are, in general, more likely to have recourse to external sources of information which may be helpful to them in acts of structuring. People are obviously the most common source of such information. Accordingly, we may expect field-independent people to function with a degree of autonomy in interpersonal relations, a tendency further encouraged by their self-nonself polarity. On the other hand, field-dependent people may be expected to function less apart from others, a tendency fostered by their continuing ties to people.

One expectation from these postulates is that, in social interaction, field-dependent people will take greater account of information from others in forming their views than will field-independent people. This expectation has been confirmed in many studies by now, although not in others. It is illuminating to compare the studies in which field-dependent and field-independent people have proven to be different in response to external referents and studies in which they were not different. Such a comparison helps define the operating variables involved in response to social referents and highlights the important role of contextual factors in determining the concrete behavioral sequelae of cognitive styles.

Studies which did find a difference between field-dependent and field-independent people employed situations which were ambiguous—that is, subjects were not given adequate information on which to base the judgment required of them. No differences have been found when unambiguous situations were used. This pattern makes sense within the framework of field-dependence theory. Under ambiguous conditions, field-dependent subjects make up for their difficulty in structuring by using information available to them from others as aids to achieving the structure required of them. When the situation has inherent structure, so that imposition of structure by the person himself is not required, field-dependent people are no different from field-independent people in their response to external social referents. The behavior of field-dependent people thus varies, in a meaningful and reasonable manner, according to the situation in which they find themselves. Field-independent people, having access to a set of internal referents and responding less to external social referents, are more constant in their behavior from situation to situation. This difference has important consequences. Field-dependent people are more likely to be aware of the views of other people and to take them into account in forming their own. Field-independent people are less likely to be attentive to others' views and may at times even disregard information from others which could actually be helpful to them.

It is worth noting that of the various behaviors discussed under dependence in the literature, only information-seeking from others seems related to field dependence-independence. Field-dependent and field-independent people are not particularly different in such other aspects of dependence as attention seeking, response to extrinsic reinforcement, approval seeking, or emotional attachment. To the extent that seeking information from others or relying on internal referents in structuring ambiguous situations is primarily responsible for the differences in interpersonal behavior between field-dependent and field-independent people, an essentially cognitive basis for that difference is suggested.

The evidence just reviewed broadens the field-dependence-independence dimension by including interpersonal behavior within it. The person who tends to rely on internal referents—that is, who is field independent—shows that tendency both in his reliance on the body as a standard for judging the upright and in his autonomy of others in social relations. The person who tends to rely on external referents—that is, who is field dependent—shows that tendency in his use of the external visual field in establishing the upright and in his recourse to standards provided by others in interpersonal situations under conditions of ambiguity.

We have thus far considered some of the direct ways in which field dependence and field independence express themselves. Through their effects on a variety of behaviors, these styles also find more indirect expression. Two consequences of the tendency to rely primarily on internal or external referents are of particular importance. First, primary reliance on internal or external referents is likely to affect the development of a more impersonal or interpersonal orientation. Second, reliance on one or the other referent is likely to influence the person's manner of dealing with cognitive tasks, particularly whether he will restructure a stimulus array on his own or follow dominant properties of the array as given. By implicating the nature of the person's social orientation and cognitive restructuring skills, the scope of the field-dependent and field-independent cognitive styles is substantially enlarged and the extent of self-consistency in behavior attributable to cognitive styles is considerably extended. Let me elaborate on the concepts of interpersonal vs. impersonal orientation and cognitive restructuring, and their place in field-dependence theory.

Field-dependent people have what may be characterized, overall, as an interpersonal orientation. That orientation has a number of ingredients, in regard to which it contrasts with the more impersonal orientation of field-independent people. I will simply list some of these ingredients now since I will be examining them in detail later on when I consider the adaptive value of each of these orientations.

Field-dependent people seek both physical and emotional closeness to others which, in turn, provides them with experience in interpersonal relations, whereas field-independent people prefer to keep others "at arm's length." Field-dependent people pay selective attention to social cues, in contrast to field-independent people who are relatively insensitive to such cues. Consistent with these differences are the characterizations of field-dependent and field-independent people that have been reported in the literature. Field-dependent people have been described as sociable, interested in people, wanting to help others, having a concern for people, knowing many people, and being known to many. Descriptions of relatively field-independent people have included individualistic, aloof, and concerned with ideas and principles rather than people.

Finally, evidence is beginning to emerge that relatively field-dependent people may be more effective than field-independent people in getting along with others. Some of their characteristics make this difference reasonable. Thus, the preference of field-dependent people for interpersonal situations provides them with greater opportunity to participate themselves, and to observe others in social-interaction situations. Their more extensive exposure to people, together with their greater sensitivity to social information, may serve to build up a fund of behavior expectancies useful in dealing with others. Field-independent people have been described in such terms as demanding, inconsiderate, and manipulative of people as a means of achieving personal ends; field-dependent people, in contrast, have more frequently been described as considerate, warm, friendly, tactful, and able to make others feel comfortable with them. Field-dependent people are also more apt to like others, and there is some evidence that they are better liked by others and are more popular as well. It is not difficult to see how these contrasting social attributes of field-dependent and field-independent people can contribute to a difference between them in ease of getting along with others.

More direct evidence is beginning to appear of the greater effectiveness of field-dependent people in interpersonal relations. That evidence comes from studies of conflict resolution. Groups including field-dependent members have been found to be more effective in reaching a consensus than groups without them. This outcome, it seems reasonable to believe, is related to the greater tendency of field-dependent people to take account of others' views and to be attentive and sensitive to others' ideas and feelings. While these characteristics are hardly sufficient conditions for working out disagreement, they do appear to be necessary conditions. It was also found in one study that conflict resolution was more often achieved by opinion shifts on the part of field-dependent than of field-independent group members. There is a suggestion here that field-independent people may be less willing or less able to accommodate their views to others' views for the sake of conflict resolution.

To summarize, it is quite clear that field-dependent people, compared to field-independent ones, give more evidence of having social behaviors and attributes useful for effective interpersonal relations, and there is some beginning evidence that they may be more effective in interpersonal relations as well. These features of field-dependent people add up to an array of what may be called interpersonal competencies which have getting along with others as their particular focus.

I turn now to the consequences of the field-dependent and field-independent cognitive styles for competence in cognitive restructuring, the second domain on which these styles have a particularly profound impact.

The internal referents available to field-independent people provide them with a fund of mediating mechanisms for use in restructuring a field on their own, when required to do so by the task at hand. Restructuring may entail organizing a field which lacks inherent structure, imposing a different organization on the field than the one it contains, or breaking up an organized field so that its parts are rendered discrete from ground. The designation "restructuring" seems appropriate for all these acts since they involve making changes in the field, or "going beyond the information given," rather than following the field "as is." When internal referents are less available, as in the case of field-dependent people, the person is more likely to respond to the dominant properties of the field as given. That field-independent people are more likely to follow a restructuring approach than field-dependent people has been demonstrated in numerous studies. These studies have examined a wide range of perceptual and problem-solving dimensions which, while discrete in particular characteristics, all require skill in cognitive restructuring. Let me enumerate some of the restructuring dimensions which have been linked to field independence.

One is disembedding, as we have called it, or flexibility of closure, as it is known in the factor-analytic literature. The best known test of this dimension is the embedded-figures test. The task here is to locate a previously seen simple figure within a larger organized geometric figure which has been designed to obscure it. The relation found between performance on tests of perception of the upright and performance on the embedded-figures test was one of the very earliest demonstrations that field independence is related to competence in cognitive restructuring. The Piagetian water-level problem, which probably also falls on the disembedding dimension, has been linked to field independence as well.

Another restructuring dimension on which field-independent people do better is speed of closure. On tests of this dimension the subject is shown an impoverished representation of an object which he is required to identify. To succeed he must provide an organization to the stimulus array.

A third restructuring dimension is "perspectivism," as Werner called it, or "decentration," the name it bears in the Piagetian literature. Perspectivism refers to the ability to recognize that the perspective another person may have of a fixed stimulus array, when viewing it from another position, may be different from one's own, and includes the additional ability to adopt the other's perspective. The three-mountain problem of Piaget is a good representative of this dimension. Successful performance on that problem has been related to field independence. Performance on standard tests of spatial-visualization ability, of the kind encountered in the factor-analytic literature, which again involves perspectivism, has been similarly related.

Restructuring in concept attainment has also been examined in relation to field independence. A distinction has long been drawn between an hypothesis testing and a spectator approach to such tasks. In the first approach the learner, adopting an active role, forms an hypothesis about the correct concept, and then applies it to the next exemplar presented to him. He proceeds in this way until he attains the correct concept. In the second approach, the learner takes a more passive role. As he encounters successive exemplars of the concept class, relevant features of the class gradually emerge and irrelevant ones fade away. As expected, field-independent people tend to use an hypothesis-testing approach in which active restructuring is required. Field-dependent people are more likely to use a spectator approach in which properties of the stimulus array itself play a dominant role.

Still other restructuring dimensions which have been related to field independence include functional fixity, perceptual constancy, set breaking, conservation, and reversible perspective.

Lest it be thought that field independence has taken an imperial hold on the entire cognitive domain, let me emphasize that measures of field independence have been found to have only a low relation, or none at all, to measures of cognitive functions that do not involve restructuring. For example, measures of perceptual speed and a number of dimensions of verbal functioning fall in this category. For the sake of establishing that it is restructuring competence in particular which is related to field independence, it has been as necessary to show that field independence is not related to dimensions which do not involve that competence as to show that it is related to dimensions which do.

In overview, the evidence, again drawn from a large literature (Witkin and Goodenough, 1976), is quite clear in showing that field-independent people are more competent in cognitive restructuring than are field-dependent people.

By way of summarizing what I have said thus far, it may be helpful to schematize the field-dependence-independence dimension along the lines of a factor-analytic structure. Imagine the model I have outlined as having a pyramidal form. At the apex of the pyramid is "differentiation." At the second level, immediately below it, is "self-nonself segregation" or field dependence-independence. At the same level in the model are "segregation of psychological functions" and "segregation of neurophysiological functions," which we have bypassed. Proceeding downward in the pyramid, at the third level below the apex, radiating from "self-nonself segregation," we have "interpersonal competencies" and "cognitive restructuring." The field-dependent and field-independent cognitive styles are, in this scheme, products of lesser or greater self-nonself segregation. In the cognitive domain, field independence expresses itself in developed competence in restructuring, and field dependence in less competence in restructuring. In the social domain, field dependence expresses itself in interpersonal competencies, field independence in less competence in interpersonal relations. Another way of casting these patterns is to say that greater self-nonself segregation makes possible reliance on internal referents which, in turn, fosters the development of cognitive restructuring skills, but does not particularly encourage the development of interpersonal competencies. On the other hand, less self-nonself segregation contributes to reliance on external referents and thereby stimulates the devclopment of interpersonal competencies, but not especially of cognitive restructuring skills. The development of relatively field-dependent and field-independent people thus follows different pathways, entailing investments in different domains.

From the account I have given of field dependence and field independence, let me now try to distill their cognitive-style essences. Although I will be using these particular cognitive styles as referents, you will not go far astray if you take the view that I am enumerating the characteristics of cognitive styles in general.

First, the field-dependent and field-independent cognitive styles are process variables. Being process variables, they represent techniques for moving toward a goal, rather than competence in achieving goals. Whether use of a particular cognitive style will contribute to goal attainment or not depends on the context in which it is used.

Second, cognitive styles are pervasive dimensions of individual functioning. They express themselves across domains traditionally considered in isolation from each other. This pervasiveness need not be surprising in the case of the field-dependent and field-independent cognitive styles, since the tendencies to rely primarily on internal or external referents, as a function of extent of self-nonself segregation, represent rather deep cuts of the psyche. We have seen that these styles manifest themselves in a wide array of cognitive functions and in many facets of interpersonal behavior. Further, in the hierarchical model of differentiation, these styles are linked to the other major manifestations of differentiation: segregation of psychological functions and segregation of neurophysiological functions. Field dependence-independence, as expected, has been shown to be related to such products of segregation of psychological functions as degree of articulation of body concept and extent of specialization of defenses. Functions ordinarily considered to be in the personality domain are thereby implicated in cognitive styles. Field dependence-independence is also linked, conceptually and empirically, to the products of segregation of neurophysiological functions.

Here, I would like to comment on recent research relating field dependence-independence to neurophysiological phenomena. This work not only extends the scope of what is implicated in cognitive styles, but it demonstrates the broad organismic character of differentiation and the power of differentiation theory to predict events in very diverse domains. Beyond that, this work opens a possible route to studying the structural basis of individual differences in cognitive style. Differentiation theory leads us to expect that one way in which greater differentiation may express itself in the neurophysiological domain is in segregation of functions. Greater segregation is likely to show itself in specialization of functions in each of the two hemispheres of the cerebral cortex. On these grounds, the hypothesis has been proposed that people who are more field independent will show greater lateralization of verbal processing in the left hemisphere, the site of processing of this kind of material, and greater lateralization of processing of configurational material in the right hemisphere, the site of that kind of processing. The hypothesis further proposes that field-dependent people are not as likely to show cerebral lateralization of either kind of functioning. You will notice that it is a difference in the degree of lateralization of functions in the two hemispheres that is predicted by differentiation theory, rather than dominance of one hemisphere over the other. The prediction that cerebral functions are likely to be more lateralized in field-independent than in field-dependent people has been confirmed in a number of studies. A dimension that can find itself at home in so many domains, now including the neurophysiological domain, is certainly pervasive.

Implicit in the concept of pervasiveness is the idea of self-consistency in individual functioning. There is, of course, no contradiction between postulating self-consistency and at the same time emphasizing the importance of contextual variables, as I have been doing. The continuity implied by self-consistency is in underlying processes rather than the outcomes of these processes. Moreover, although the outcomes vary with context, they too are predictable from knowledge of the individual's cognitive style, the nature of the situation, and the interaction between them. Thus, knowing the emphasis field-dependent people place on the external visual field as a referent and knowing the position of the field in relation to the true upright in a given instance, we can foretell that such a person will come out with a generally accurate determination of the upright in the rotating-room test, where the visual field is straight, but with a quite inaccurate determination in the rod-and-frame and body-adjustment tests, where the field is tilted. From a person-situation-interaction perspective, the outcome of use of a particular cognitive style under specified conditions is "lawful," and hence predictable.

A third characteristic of cognitive styles is that they tend to be stable. They thus show consistency over time as well as across domains. This means that from knowledge of an individual's cognitive style at one time we can predict his cognitive style at a later time with reasonable accuracy. That cognitive styles do show a fair degree of stability need not be surprising when we recall that they are the products of formal properties of the organism. We would not expect content variables to show comparable stability. In saying that cognitive styles tend to be stable over time, I do not mean to imply that they are unchangeable. As we shall see later, evidence from training studies suggests that the development of at least some components of the field-dependence-independence dimension may be influenced by specially designed educational efforts.

A fourth characteristic of cognitive styles is that they are bipolar. As we have seen, field-dependent people show interpersonal competencies, particularly those likely to figure in getting along with others, but they do not do well in situations requiring cognitive restructuring. In contrast, field-independent people do well in cognitive restructuring situations but give less evidence of interpersonal competencies. The cluster of restructuring skills and the cluster of interpersonal competencies thus have their high and low levels at opposite poles of the field-dependence-independence cognitive-style dimension. It is in this sense that the dimension is bipolar.

The bipolarity of cognitive styles is responsible for still another of their characteristics. This fifth characteristic of cognitive styles is that they are value-neutral. Each pole of the field-dependence-independence dimension has qualities that may help a person to get along in specified circumstances. Accordingly, whether a given cognitive style is "good" or "bad" depends on its adaptive value in a particular situation. It is not inherently better or worse to be located toward one pole of the field-dependence-independence dimension or the other. For cognitive styles value is relative to context.

The bipolarity and value-neutral stance of cognitive styles are undoubtedly their most distinctive features. It is these features, which, most of all, set them apart from other dimensions, such as abilities, which are characteristically unipolar with regard to level and biased with regard to value. These features also make it possible for cognitive styles to serve adaptive ends. We now turn to this issue.

TWO

Cognitive Styles in Human Adaptation

Because the field-dependent and field-independent cognitive styles are different in their adaptive consequences, it need not be surprising that people develop cognitive styles which are adaptive to the demands of the life situations with which they must cope. Conversely, cognitive styles have been shown to cause people to gravitate toward life situations to which their styles are suited. Achievement of adaptive correspondence between cognitive styles and life circumstances is thus a two-way street. Moreover, reflecting their salience as a developmental force, cognitive styles guide the formation of modes of behavior in people which are compatible with their styles. And, finally, a person's cognitive style may influence others to behave toward him in a manner which suits his cognitive style and is thereby helpful to him in his interpersonal relations. I want to consider examples of each of these kinds of adaptive attunement in turn.

✿　✿　✿　✿　✿

Attunement of Cognitive Styles to Life Situations

I start with the issue of attunement between people's cognitive styles and the demands placed on them by their life's circumstances. I propose to consider attunement as it occurs during individual ontogenetic development and as it probably occurred in the course of development of cultural forms from earlier hunting-based economies to later agriculture-based economies. The evidence I draw upon comes from a large body of cross-cultural research on cognitive styles conducted with groups from many different parts of the world. I will focus on subsistence-level groups because, in several ways, they are particularly useful for an examination of the attunement issue. The ecological forces to which they are subjected, and to which they must adjust, are potent and pervasive. The pressure to adapt is strong, since survival itself is at issue. The life requirements against which the adaptive value of cognitive styles may be examined are therefore easily identifiable.

Let me note in passing that in this cross-cultural work, and in many of the other areas we will consider in our discussion of the role of cognitive styles in adaptation, we are dealing with real-life situations. An opportunity is thus afforded to take cognitive styles out of the laboratory, where they had their beginnings, and to examine their implications for everyday life.

The cross-cultural studies I want to consider compared cognitive styles of subsistence-level migratory hunting and gathering groups, on the one hand, with sedentary agricultural groups, on the other hand. These two kinds of groups present a sharply contrasting picture in the behaviors they require for the conduct of their economies. Furthermore, the behaviors adaptive to each kind of economy correspond closely to the characteristics of field-independent and field-dependent people. The specific hypothesis which stimulated the earliest work in this area and which, in more complex form, has guided it ever since, is that members of migratory groups are likely to be relatively field independent and members of sedentary groups relatively field dependent.

The expectation of attunement between a group's modal cognitive style and the demands of its life setting, implied in this hypothesis, appears plausible when we compare some of the salient features of a migratory hunting-gathering existence and a sedentary agricultural existence with the characteristics of relatively field-dependent and field-independent people. The features of each kind of existence constitute a cluster of closely interrelated ecological, child-rearing, and cultural characteristics fashioned by the group's mode of economic exploitation of its surroundings.

The migratory existence followed by hunters in gaining their livelihood requires them to find their way around their environment—usually an environment which is visually homogeneous, such as the flat snowlands of the Eskimo or the uniform desert terrain of the Arunta. Structure must, accordingly, be given to fields which have little inherent articulation. Moreover, locating food often requires extracting and using small bits of information from the environment, in other words, analytical functioning. In these and other ways, developed cognitive restructuring skills are important to the hunter if he is to survive. Such skills are of much less moment to the agriculturalist for the economic activities he conducts in his sedentary existence.

As another difference, hunters typically live in small bands and expect members of the band to be "jacks-of-all-trades"; role diversity is thus limited. Each person is expected to be able to do many things on his own and, particularly among solitary hunters, to fend for himself on the hunt. Agriculturalists, as a consequence of their sedentary existence, made possible by the local availability of food, typically live in larger groups with more elaborate social structures and greater role diversity. Compared to the life of a hunter, the close group living of agriculturalists entails more social commerce with a greater variety of people and more emphasis on the ability to get along with others. Continued connectedness with others is thus encouraged and the development of interpersonal competencies likely to be fostered.

Hunters and agriculturalists also differ in their manner of using the products of their exploitative modes. Whereas hunters typically consume their catch, and go out on another hunt when it is depleted, agriculturalists conserve their farm products between harvests.

In view of the quite different characteristics required to conduct hunting and agricultural economies effectively, it need not be surprising that the social structures and child-rearing practices found among hunters and agriculturalists are different in ways calculated to produce the kinds of people needed for each.

With regard to social structure, migratory hunting societies may best be described as "loose" and agricultural societies as "tight" (Pelto, 1968). The loose societies characteristic of migratory groups typically have little social, political, or religious structure. The tight societies characteristic of sedentary groups have elaborate social structures, marked social stratification, and considerable role diversity; conformity to social, religious, and political authority is stressed, and adherence to authority is strongly enforced. The tight-loose distinction is also evident in the characteristic differences in child-rearing practices between hunting and agricultural groups. Mobile hunting groups are tolerant of children's violations of adult authority and, instead, emphasize self-reliance and autonomy. Among agriculturalists, on the other hand, compliance with parental authority is emphasized in child-rearing, much as compliance to political, social, and religious authority is stressed in society at large. It is not difficult to see how tight social organization and child-rearing for conformity can serve the needs of agricultural groups to exercise control over individual behavior in their larger and more complex societies and to regulate food consumption between harvests. Nor is it difficult to see how a loose social structure, and the encouragement of autonomy and self-reliance in child-rearing, can serve the needs of hunting groups for individuals who can fend for themselves in the mobile existence they lead during the search for game.

Quite evidently, under the subsistence-level conditions we have been considering, ecology, social structure, and socialization practices work in tandem towards the same developmental end of producing modes of behavior that are adaptive to a migratory hunting existence or a sedentary agricultural existence. These interrelated variables have been combined by Berry (1976) into an ecocultural dimension, characterized at one extreme by a nomadic hunting-gathering existence, loose social organization, and socialization for autonomy, and, at the other extreme, by a sedentary agricultural existence, tight social organization, and socialization for conformity.

If there is indeed attunement between people's cognitive styles and the requirements of their life settings, we may expect to find a correspondence between a group's standing on the ecocultural dimension and its standing on the field-dependence-independence dimension. Consider some of the key concepts in the account just given of typical hunting and agricultural groups, and, at the same time, recall some of the key concepts in my earlier account of field-independent and field-dependent people. On the side of both hunters and field-independent people we find an emphasis on cognitive restructuring skills and personal autonomy, with less emphasis on interpersonal competencies. On the side of both agriculturalists and field-dependent people, we find an emphasis on the competencies important in interpersonal relations, as well as on connectedness with others, and only limited emphasis on cognitive restructuring skills.

The expectation that members of mobile groups would be more field independent than members of sedentary groups has received substantial support from numerous studies (Witkin and Berry, 1975). It is particularly impressive that the same pattern, encompassing ecology, social structure, socialization, and cognitive style, has appeared repeatedly among mobile hunting groups from widely separated parts of the world which probably never had contact with each other—for example, the Arunta of Australia, the Boat People of Hong Kong, the Cree, Athabaskan, Ojibway and Carrier Amerindians, the Lapps, and the Canadian, Greenlandic, and Alaskan Eskimos. The contrasting pattern has been found among equally scattered sedentary agricultural groups—for example, Southern Nigerians, the Temne and Mende of Sierra Leone, the Nsenga of Zambia, South African Bantu, Tsimshian Amerindians, the Haka of Hong Kong, and Fijian Islanders. These findings seem to support the thesis that how people make their living is important in determining not only the social forms they adopt, but also the child-rearing practices they develop and the patterns of individual behavior they encourage. Perhaps this thesis finds particularly impressive support in the subsistence-level settings we have been considering because economic factors hold such great sway in these settings.

The evidence that a field-dependent or field-independent cognitive style is commonplace in the ecological context to which it is suited supports the view that people's cognitive styles develop in accord with the requirements of their life situations. The question needs to be addressed, however, of how this fit is achieved in the course of ontogenetic development. First, we may look to the role of socialization. The child-rearing practices found in hunting societies are strikingly similar to those which have been found to foster the development of a field-independent cognitive style among individuals within cultures, Western and non-Western alike. What is central in these practices is the encouragement of self-nonself segregation and, thereby, the development of internal frames of reference or a field-independent cognitive style. Such a style makes possible competence in cognitive restructuring and personal autonomy, both of which are so advantageous in a hunting setting. Correspondingly, the child-rearing practices common to agricultural societies are similar to those which studies conducted within cultures, both Western and non-Western, have shown to stimulate the development of a field-dependent cognitive style. Critical here is the encouragement of continued self-other connectedness which fosters the development of a field-dependent cognitive style and, with it, the interpersonal skills and social characteristics likely to be useful in an agricultural setting.

A second source of factors contributing to the development of cognitive styles in attunement with the individual's life setting may be found in prevailing cultural arrangements. The loose and tight social organizations characteristic of hunting and agricultural societies work in tandem with child-rearing practices within the family to influence development toward greater or lesser self-nonself segregation.

Finally, direct encounters with the ecology provide still another source of factors contributing to the development of cognitive styles attuned to ecological requirements. Take the hunting setting and consider the growing child as he increasingly engages himself in what is usually a homogeneous environment in the search for game. That engagement, which, as we have seen, requires analysis and structuring of his uniform surroundings, is likely to contribute to the development of cognitive restructuring skills. Parents may participate in this process of perceptual training, of course. They may do so, for example, by imparting to their child a vocabulary which may be helpful in the restructuring process. A Pygmy hunting group we are now studying in the Central African Republic, in comparison to a sedentary group of Bantu agriculturalists, is reputed to have as many words for the vegetation in the deep, dark forest in which they hunt as do professional botanists. It is not difficult to see how having words for specific components of one's surroundings may help make these components discrete, thereby converting the rough-grained homogeneous forest environment into a more articulated field.

In these ways, then, socialization, culture, and ecological encounters may collaborate to bring about the attunement we find in hunting and agricultural groups between cognitive style and demands of the ecological setting.

That both a field-dependent and field-independent cognitive style may be adaptive in specified contexts provides a particularly impressive demonstration of their value-neutral character. This feature makes work with these cognitive styles congenial to the cross-cultural enterprise. In particular, it provides a countervailing force to the risks of ethnocentrism commonly encountered when concepts and dimensions developed in one culture are then transferred to other cultures. A particularly common source of ethnocentric bias lies in the incorporation into a concept or dimension of the value emphases peculiar to the original culture. In the case of cognitive styles, there is no advance assignment of higher value status to one cognitive style over another, or to the cognitive style typical of one culture over that of another culture. Defining value according to context, as cognitive-style theory proposes, diminishes the intrusion of value as a source of ethnocentric bias. By drawing attention to local conditions as a basis for value judgments, such a relativist position discourages advance assignment of higher status to whatever is Western in origin.

The bipolar conception of cognitive styles makes it not at all surprising that there is no clear Western-non-Western ordering on the field-dependence-independence dimension. In the evidence now on hand, means for these groups on such tests as the embedded-figures test, Block Design, and the rod-and-frame test do not appear to be appreciably different. Just as non-Western groups show considerable diversity among themselves as a function of their standing on the ecocultural dimension, so do Western groups show diversity as a function of their social structures and socialization practices.

To this point we have been looking at the development of cognitive styles as individual adaptations, during ontogeny, to the requirements of a sedentary agricultural or a mobile hunting existence. The attunement between cognitive styles and ecological demands may also be considered from an historic perspective. It seems quite clear that earlier—in fact probably over as much as 99 percent of human history—people lived as hunters and food gatherers and only recently shifted to a farming and pastoral existence. This change in mode of economic exploitation is likely to have been accompanied by changes in cultural forms. While we have no direct way of knowing the course of development of cognitive styles over the period of change in cultural forms, the evidence from the studies of contemporary hunting and agricultural groups we just reviewed does allow us to draw some inferences. These studies have shown a field-independent cognitive style to be commonly associated with a hunting existence and a field-dependent cognitive style with an agricultural existence; and the development of each of these styles seems to be a response to the adaptive pressures of the ecological setting in which it is found. It seems reasonable to believe that similar adaptive pressures were operative during human cultural development, with similar consequences. The studies of contemporary groups also have shown that the development of a field-independent and field-dependent style in hunting and agricultural groups is closely linked to the interrelated cluster of ecological, societal, and child-rearing influences that produce the cognitive styles characteristic of each of these groups. Since the components of each are interrelated in a highly meaningful way, it is reasonable to believe that they were interrelated in a similar fashion during the history of cultural development. These inferences seem particularly plausible when we consider that, both over the course of history and during ontogeny, the developments we are considering took place under the pressure of a subsistence-level existence. So, if we extrapolate from the evidence obtained in presently existing hunting and agricultural groups, we are led to the proposal that, with the transition from hunting-based to agricultural-based cultural

field-dependent cognitive style can thus be seen as being more adaptive for women in subsistence-level sedentary groups than for women in migratory groups. This may be one basis for the more pronounced sex differences in field dependence-independence in sedentary agricultural groups.

Another closely related basis may lie in the differential value attached to women's participation in the primary economic mode in the two kinds of ecocultural settings. All societies assign somewhat different roles in subsistence activities to men and women. In smaller, more mobile, less stratified hunting societies, with their limited role diversity, however, the contribution of all its members, both women and men, is valued that much more highly than in role-diverse sedentary groups. With greater value placed on women's part in the economy, there is likely to be greater allowance of autonomy—in other words, greater self-nonself segregation and a more field-independent cognitive style.

In view of the nature of women's role in the subsistence-level activities of hunting groups, a more field-independent cognitive style may be seen as adaptive for them much as the greater emphasis on social activities among women in agricultural groups makes a more field-dependent cognitive style adaptive for them. Here again we have evidence of the suitability of each of these cognitive styles to particular life circumstances. Clearly, characteristics of the ecocultural context serve as moderator variables in determining the nature and extent of sex differences in cognitive styles.

✽ ✽ ✽ ✽ ✽

Choice of Life Situations Adaptive to Cognitive Styles

To this point we have examined one route by which attunement between cognitive styles and the demands of life circumstances may be achieved: through the development of cognitive styles that are adaptive to specified life conditions. Now, we consider the achievement of attune-

be somewhat more field independent than women is very likely a product of the greater emphasis on self-nonself segregation in raising boys than girls in Western settings. To the extent that socialization is the operative variable, by reversing this emphasis it should be possible to reverse the sex difference now commonly found.

Indeed, cross-cultural studies have shown that sex differences in field dependence-independence are not as common in non-Western settings as they have proved to be in Western settings. More important, the non-Western studies have begun to identify some of the reasons for the presence or absence of sex differences. Where significantly greater field dependence in females than in males is found, it is largely in samples from the sedentary-agricultural end of the ecocultural dimension. Significant sex differences tend to be absent from groups at the mobile-hunting end. It seems possible to understand this pattern by considering the adaptive demands placed upon boys and girls as they grow up in each of these contrasting ecocultural settings. For reasons I suggested earlier, the requirements of close, large-group living typical of sedentary groups are likely to foster the development of social conformity and interpersonal competencies in both sexes, at the expense of individual autonomy, more typical of migratory groups. In addition, the characteristically greater social complexity of the physically static and larger agricultural groups makes for more social roles, among all of its members. As we have seen, the smaller size and frequent change of locale of nomadic groups require that their members be able to do more or less all of the things required for the group's survival, often on their own. Greater role diversity in sedentary groups includes greater differences between male and female roles. Moreover, the specialized roles defined for women involve more exclusive preoccupation with child-related activities and nurturance. The stronger interpersonal orientation fostered among all members of the group is likely to be emphasized even more for women in their family-care roles. The social characteristics of a

erties is adaptive in a particular life context. In the case of ontogenetic development, reliance on external referents in information processing, or a field-dependent cognitive style, seems suitable to the young child's relation to other people and to his psychological and physical makeup as well. Reliance on internal referents, or a field-independent cognitive style, and, as part of it, relative autonomy of others and skill in cognitive restructuring seem more suited to adult status. The overall trend in ontogenetic development towards greater field independence leaves room, however, for diversity among adults in the extent to which their personal development fosters the sharpening of personal autonomy or of interpersonal skills and of greater or less cognitive restructuring skills. In the case of development over the course of human history, a field-independent cognitive style was clearly adaptive to the earlier mobile hunting economic mode, and a field-dependent cognitive style was adaptive to the later sedentary agricultural mode. Cognitive-style theory thus provides a common conceptual framework for predicting the likely progression in diverse developmental series.

There is an additional body of work reported in the cross-cultural research on cognitive styles which provides another instance of the development of cognitive styles towards attunement with the demands of life circumstances—the work on sex differences.

As background for the cross-cultural research on sex differences, it should be noted that many studies in the United States and in other Western countries have reported a sex difference in field dependence-independence, although the difference probably does not become regular or persistent until somewhere around early adolescence. The tendency is for women to be more field dependent than men. The difference between the sexes is quite small; the range within each sex is vastly greater than the difference between the sexes. It should be emphasized, in this regard, that the existence of sex differences is not a postulate of field-dependence theory. The tendency for men to

forms, there also took place a change from a more field-independent cognitive style towards a more field-dependent cognitive style.

In speculating about how the attunement between cognitive styles and ecological demands was brought about over the course of cultural history, we may appeal to the same operative variables which seem responsible for the similar attunement found during ontogeny. Adaptive selection may be conceived to have favored the societal arrangements and child-rearing procedures typical of contemporary sedentary cultural groups over the societal arrangements and child-rearing procedures previously more common in a hunting ecology. Through phenotypic transmission, operating over the long haul of history, adaptive selection produced the relatively more field-dependent cognitive style suited to the emerging agricultural existence.

The evidence from cross-sectional and longitudinal studies makes it quite clear that the trend in ontogenetic development is from relative field dependence to greater field independence. This is true of both Western and non-Western groups. At the same time, we have inferred that the trend of development of cultural forms has been from relative field independence towards greater field dependence. That developmental progressions may take opposite pathways during ontogeny and over the course of human history is entirely consistent with the bipolar conception of cognitive styles, although running counter to premises implicit in some developmental theories. For cognitive styles, as I have been suggesting, a driving force in their development is achievement of fit between cognitive styles and the demands of life situations. Because each pole of the field-dependent-independent cognitive-style dimension has adaptive properties, prevailing life demands may foster development towards one pole or the other. The direction that the development of cognitive styles is likely to take in any particular developmental progression depends on which of the alternative sets of prop-

ment by the opposite route: through the selection of life situations compatible with a person's cognitive style. I will use two examples to illustrate this route to attunement. One is the choice of educational-vocational domains suited to the person's cognitive style; the other is the choice of people who are similar in cognitive style, and therefore likely to be congenial, to share important life situations.

The sizable literature (Witkin, Moore, Goodenough, and Cox, 1977) on the role of cognitive styles in career differentiation has made it quite clear that relatively field-independent students are likely to be interested in and to choose educational and vocational pursuits that call for cognitive restructuring skills, but are not especially social in their content or require relations with others for their conduct. In contrast, relatively field-dependent students are likely to favor pursuits which have a "people" emphasis —that is, which feature social content, involve relations with others, and do not emphasize cognitive restructuring skills. Reflecting the bipolarity of the field dependence-independence cognitive-style dimension, each kind of student moves toward domains for which his cognitive and social characteristics are particularly suited.

To give content to these generalizations, let me specify some of the areas which field-dependent and field-independent students have been found to favor. Considering interests, studies have shown with fair regularity that responses of field-independent people on interest inventories are consistent with those of persons in the domains of mathematics and the natural sciences, of teachers of agricultural and industrial subjects, of health professionals such as physicians and dentists, and of people in practical occupations such as foresters and farmers. They give evidence as well of being interested in the theoretical, the abstract, and the artistic. In contrast, the cluster of interests frequently found among field-dependent people includes elementary-school and social-science teaching, business administration, the welfare-helping-humanitarian professions, such as social work and the ministry, administrative activities which require dealing with people, such as personnel direction, and persuasive activities, such as selling. As is to be expected, the results of studies of educational-vocational choices are very much in line with those of the interest studies. In the academic setting, relatively field-independent college and graduate students are likely to favor such fields as the natural sciences, mathematics, art, engineering, and experimental psychology. Relatively field-dependent students are likely to favor such fields as elementary-school teaching, social work, clinical psychology, and religion. The results of studies of people already engaged in their chosen occupations are consistent with these findings. Note, too, that persons with contrasting cognitive styles are not especially different with regard to the social-status value of their preferences and choices. In this respect, again, cognitive styles are value-neutral.

The studies of attunement between people's cognitive styles and the educational-vocational domains they favor have almost invariably been cross-sectional in nature. A longitudinal study we did sought to overcome some of the limitations of cross-sectional studies. First, following the academic development of the same students over an extended period of time gives us a better chance to identify the processes through which attunement is achieved. Second, a longitudinal study provides a better opportunity to distinguish cause and effect in the attunement process. In most of the cross-sectional studies on record, the cognitive styles of subjects were assessed after they were already engaged in their chosen academic majors or vocations. The possibility cannot be excluded that performance on the cognitive-style tests reflected, in some degree, experience with the chosen domain. In our longitudinal study, students were tested for cognitive style when they first embarked on their academic careers. This makes it reasonable to assume that subsequent events in their careers were influenced by their cognitive styles rather than the other way around.

The subjects in the longitudinal study were the entire entering class of a large municipal college. In addition to assessing their cognitive styles at college entry, information was also obtained about their preliminary major choices, their vocational plans, and their Scholastic Aptitude Test scores. At college graduation, their final college majors were determined; and for those who went on to graduate or professional school, the area of specialization at this advanced level was established. With these data we were able to examine choices made by the same students at three separate points in their academic careers in relation to cognitive style: at college admission, college graduation, and graduate or professional school entry. For this examination we composed two clusters of majors corresponding in their emphases to the characteristics found towards the opposite poles of the field-dependence-independence cognitive-style dimension. One, a Science cluster, included the natural sciences and mathematics, and was expected to be favored by more field-independent students. The other, an Education cluster, included mainly elementary education, but also early childhood education, speech therapy, and nursing. We expected this cluster to be favored by more field-dependent students. At all three points in the students' academic careers the expected relationship was observed.

We found, in addition, that cognitive styles related more strongly to students' final college majors and graduate/professional school specialties than to the preliminary major preferences they expressed at college entry. This was a pattern we anticipated from the conception that people are likely to move into life situations compatible with their cognitive styles. In the present context this meant that students whose preliminary choices at college entry were congruent with their cognitive styles could be expected to remain with these choices through their academic careers. On the other hand, students with initially incongruent choices could be expected to shift, over time, to more compatible domains. This is just what we found.

Field-dependent students who chose mathematics or the natural sciences as majors at college entry tended to shift from their original majors, by college graduation or graduate school entry, into other more congenial majors. Field-independent students who chose these same majors at the outset tended to stay with them. An opposite pattern was found for majors in the Education cluster. Among students with majors in that cluster it was rather the field-independent students who tended to shift and the field-dependent ones to remain. That among preliminary Science majors the most field-independent ones are likely to remain in their chosen field, whereas among preliminary Education majors the most field-dependent ones are likely to remain, is in line with the bipolarity of the field-dependence-independence cognitive-style dimension. So we see that there is a spontaneously occurring process in students' academic lives which, over time, brings about a better fit between their cognitive styles and the areas they select for study and work. It seems reasonable to postulate that this better attunement is achieved through the experiences students have in courses within their chosen specialty and in early-level courses outside their specialty.

The phenomenon of stability or shift in students' majors, as a function of congruence or incongruence between major and cognitive style, has obvious practical consequences in the educational setting. Knowledge about a student's cognitive style, at the time of entry into college, can help predict whether he is likely to earn his degree in that major, and, beyond that, whether he is likely to specialize in it should he go on to graduate school. In fact, our study showed that cognitive styles contribute to such predictions above and beyond the contribution made by predictors now in common use. These include major preference at college entry and aptitude measures derived from the Verbal and Mathematics components of the Scholastic Aptitude Test.

Thus far we have considered the relation between cognitive styles and educational-vocational choices. What about the relation between cognitive styles and achievement? To begin with, reflecting the bipolar nature of the field-dependence-independence cognitive-style dimension, measures of that dimension show little relation to such overall achievement indicators as college grade-point average. However, as may be expected from the difference in academic choices they make, field-dependent and field-independent students are likely to earn their similar grade-point averages in different mixtures of courses. In line with this picture, there is some evidence that people are likely to do better in academic and vocational specialties to which their cognitive styles suit them.

Most studies in the academic setting have shown, as expected, that field-independent students are likely to do better than field-dependent students in such fields as the natural sciences, mathematics, architecture, and engineering. Little evidence is as yet available on performance in academic domains in which field-dependent people may be expected to do better. This is in part because attention to the social sphere is a relatively recent addition to field-dependence theory.

Evidence from the vocational domain, although quite sparse, is consistent with expectations. Let me cite just one example. A study done with student nurses showed that those nurses who did well in psychiatry were relatively field dependent; those who did well in surgery were relatively field independent. It is not difficult to see how the interpersonal competencies of the more field-dependent student nurses would stand them in good stead in the interpersonal relations so critical to effective care of psychiatric patients. Correspondingly, the cognitive restructuring skills of the more field-independent nurses are likely to have benefited them in the technical tasks nurses face in the fast-moving operating-room scene, where interpersonal competencies are not likely to matter much. That both field-dependent and field-independent people may do well in vocational pursuits to which their cognitive styles are adaptive is another sign of the value-neutral character of these styles.

I turn now to a second example of how attunement may be achieved through the selection of life situations which are congenial to the person's cognitive style. This example involves the tendency of people to select others similar to themselves in cognitive style to share important life situations with them. I have chosen to examine it, even though it has received relatively little research attention as yet. I do so, first, because it takes the issue of attunement into the important domain of interpersonal relations, and, second, because I believe the area offers rich possibilities for productive research.

There is now a sizable literature which suggests that people matched to each other in cognitive style are more likely than mismatched people to develop interpersonal attraction during social interactions. This match-mismatch effect has now been demonstrated with good consistency in patient-therapist, teacher-student, and peer interactions. The only studies in this group that bear upon our present interest are those which used situations in which the person actually had the option to choose or abandon another.

Two of the relevant studies examined college students' choices of roommates. One of these was conducted with second-year students, all men, at a small private college where, at the beginning of that year, students are for the first time allowed to choose a roommate rather than having him assigned. Scores on tests of field dependence-independence of the students who selected each other as roommates showed a substantial and significant correlation. A similar study, conducted at a different college by another investigator, now with women students, took the issue a step further by seeing how matters stood between roommate dyads who had already spent a year living together. Students were asked at the end of the year whether they wished to room together again or preferred to separate. The correlation of field-dependence test scores for dyads who chose to continue living together was positive, the correlation for those who chose to separate was negative; and the difference between the correlations was significant. For a third example I turn to the therapy situation and consider the main free choice available to the patient: to quit. In this study significantly more patients treated by therapists dissimilar to them in cognitive style had dropped out by the end of two months of therapy, compared to patients treated by therapists with similar cognitive styles.

My final example comes from still a different social-interaction context: selection of each other by members of the opposite sex. One study has shown that men and women students currently in college who were married, living together, or dating each other exclusively showed significant correlations in their field-dependence test scores. Several other studies with married couples did not find such a relation, however. It may be relevant to this difference in outcome that the study which found a relation was conducted recently with couples who had just come together, whereas the studies which found no relation tested in the present couples who had married fifteen or twenty years ago. It has been suggested that nowadays choice of mates is more likely to be based on how they hit it off personally with each other, thereby implicating cognitive styles, than was true earlier when such externals as "being a good provider" and "coming from a good family" were more likely to have mattered. The selection of mates on the basis of similarity in cognitive style may be a relatively recent development.

Although the evidence from these diverse social-interaction contexts is not fully consistent, there is enough to suggest that we are probably dealing with a real phenomenon. To the extent that people congruent in cognitive style tend to be similar in interests, personality characteristics, and communication modes, interaction between them is likely to be easier than in the absence of such similarities. On these grounds, gravitating towards others of a similar cognitive style, when life presents that opportunity—and, by the same token, moving away from those who are dissimilar—may be seen as adaptive and, consequently, as contributing to attunement between cognitive styles and life settings.

❄   ❄   ❄   ❄   ❄

Development of Behaviors Adaptive to Cognitive Styles

Thus far we have considered attunement between cognitive styles and a person's life circumstances, as achieved either by development of cognitive styles adaptive to the demands of life situations or by the selection of life situations suited to the person's cognitive style. I turn now to another kind of attunement: between cognitive style and behaviors of the person that are adaptive to his cognitive style. To illustrate this kind of attunement, I pick up and develop in more detail a theme touched upon earlier when characterizing the field-dependent and field-independent cognitive styles. As noted then, because internal referents are not as available to them, field-dependent people are less able to structure situations on their own and so are likely to look to information from others as guides to structuring situations which lack it. In other words, field-dependent people tend to be information seekers under ambiguous conditions. Because field-independent people have recourse to internal referents in structuring situations which lack it, they are able to function more autonomously of others. The tendencies to be autonomous or to rely more upon others are expressions of the field-dependent and field-independent cognitive styles in the social domain and so are integral components of these styles. In discussing the social aspects of field dependence and field independence I also listed a variety of differences in social behaviors between people with these contrasting styles. Furthermore, I suggested that these behaviors add up to an interpersonal orientation in the case of field-dependent people and an impersonal orientation in the case of field-independent people.

The proposal now to be made is that these social behaviors help the individual meet the requirements set by his cognitive style and in that sense are adaptive to his style. The behaviors constituting the interpersonal orientation of field-dependent people help give them access to information from others when they need it as aids to structuring. The behaviors making up the impersonal orientation of field-independent people contribute to the maintenance of separateness from others which their cognitive style allows. It seems plausible that the specific social behaviors we find associated with a particular cognitive style develop under the aegis of that style so as to bring about the adaptive attunement we find. However, longitudinal studies are needed to check this proposition. It is further possible that once these social behaviors are established, they may acquire some degree of functional autonomy.

Let us examine the interpersonal characteristics of field-dependent people which seem to serve the adaptive requirements of their cognitive style by giving them access to information from others when they need it and the impersonal characteristics of field-independent people, which seem attuned to their cognitive style and which make information from others less important.

First, field-dependent people pay selective attention to social cues from their surroundings. Field-independent people are relatively inattentive to social cues. This difference is manifested in a variety of ways and under a wide range of circumstances. One impressive manifestation of field-dependent people's greater attentiveness to social cues is found in their looking behavior. During social interaction they are more likely than field-independent people to direct their gaze at the face—or even the eyes—of the person with whom they are interacting. Obviously, at times when information from another is needed, the face of the other is a particularly good place to look. Looking at faces is especially pronounced among field-dependent people when they encounter difficulty with the task confronting them and when the person with whom they are interacting is a likely source of cues for dealing with the problem at hand. If these conditions are not met, differences in looking behavior between field-dependent and field-independent people are not likely to occur.

In the work on looking behavior, we find particularly dramatic examples of how the same stylistic tendencies may lead to different—and even opposite—concrete behaviors, depending on situational demands. In the studies which produced the evidence just cited, the subject was allowed to look wherever he wished. There have been other studies in which the subject was instructed to maintain eye contact with the experimenter while carrying out two different kinds of tasks in his head—at one time tasks which called for considerable cognitive processing or emotionally charged imagery, at another time tasks which required minimal cognitive processing. With the difficult tasks, field-dependent subjects showed more breaking of eye contact than did field-independent subjects. No difference was found with the easy tasks. Breaking eye contact during the performance of difficult mental operations has been interpreted as the need to clear channel space in order to allow internal processing. To the extent that others' faces engage the attention of field-dependent people so strongly, it may be especially important for them to avoid looking at others' faces if they are to deal effectively with the demanding mental task they must perform. These opposite behaviors among field-dependent people—avoiding others' faces when engaged in internal processing of difficult cognitive material and looking at faces when they are likely to benefit from the information they may obtain there—both reflect the special tug of faces upon their attention. So once again we find that the concrete behavioral sequelae of use of a given cognitive style may vary with context.

The keying of the attention of field-dependent people to social cues is hardly limited to faces. It is evident in the medium of verbal communication as well. A number of studies have used an incidental learning paradigm to check on subjects' recall and recognition of verbal material which was present in the periphery of attention while they were carrying out an assigned focal task. In most of these studies, field-dependent subjects recognized and recalled significantly more words with social connotations than did field-independent subjects. No difference was found with neutral words. The radar-like pursuit of social cues by field-dependent people is thus robust enough to pick them up even when they have been made weak and irrelevant by being placed out of the range of focal attention.

It seems clear from this evidence on social sensitivity that field-dependent people are in better touch with social aspects of their environment than are field-independent people.

There is a second way in which field-dependent people may acquire access to information from others. That is by spending their time with others, and even near others, in contrast to field-independent persons who favor solitary, impersonal situations and who prefer to maintain their distance from others. Being among others, it seems reasonable to assume, should facilitate the acquisition of social cues to which field-dependent people are sensitive. Most studies of the use of interpersonal space have shown that field-dependent people prefer to be physically near to those with whom they interact, as compared to field-independent people. This has been demonstrated by such simple procedures as measuring the distance at which the subject placed himself from the person with whom he was in conversation. It has also been demonstrated by more subtle means. One study examined nonverbal behavior in patients when seated at a two-foot and a five-foot distance from the therapist. At the greater distance, field-dependent patients showed more gestures loading a "dependency factor" than they did at the smaller distance. These gestures included mouth touching, lip and tongue activity, and palms-up gestures. Field-independent patients were unaffected by the distance manipulation. Physical closeness seems particularly helpful in the acquisition of the detailed cues available in the other person's facial expressions and gestures.

An especially impressive example of the difference between field-dependent and field-independent people in their preferences for interpersonal or more solitary situations is provided by the evidence on the educational-vocational choices we have already examined. Similar evidence has come from observations of children in nursery schools. Most of the studies here have shown that relatively field-dependent youngsters spend more of their time in social play and relatively field-independent youngsters in solitary play. These findings are important for their suggestion that preference for impersonal or interpersonal situations, as a function of cognitive style, begins to emerge very early in life.

There is a third area of social behavior which distinguishes field-dependent from field-independent people, and which may affect their access to information from others. This difference is in their manner of handling hostility. A number of studies have shown that field-independent people are able to express hostile feelings and aggression directly against another person, whereas field-dependent people avoid expressing hostility in this form. This difference is specifically limited to what they do with feelings of hostility once aroused; they do not differ in their capacity to experience such feelings, in acknowledging their presence, or in recognizing hostility in others. To the extent that field-dependent people rely on external social referents, acting aggressively against others may jeopardize—or at least may be perceived by them as jeopardizing—the relations on which they rely. Field-independent people, because of their greater autonomy, do not run such a risk. The difference between field-dependent and field-independent people in their readiness to express aggression directly against others may be due to differences in the way they were socialized. Parents of relatively field-dependent children are more likely to socialize against the expression of aggressive behavior—particularly when directed against the parents themselves—than are parents of relatively field-independent children.

One source of evidence on the expression of hostility is a group of studies which, by experimental means, produced hostile feelings in the subject, who was afterwards given the opportunity to express these feelings by acting against another person. These studies allowed assessment of outwardly-directed hostility in observable behavior. Field-independent subjects more commonly showed hostile behavior under these conditions than did field-dependent people. Another study was similar in design to these, but differed in providing the subject an indirect outlet for his feelings—responding to a written questionnaire—rather than the direct outlet of acting against another person. With this more indirect channel for expressing hostility available to them, field-dependent subjects were no different from field-independent ones in frequency of hostile criticism of the experimenter and the task. The tendency of field-dependent people to avoid expressing hostility directly against others has obvious implications for the maintenance of continuing interpersonal relations.

In summary, field-dependent and field-independent people seem to develop behaviors adaptive to their cognitive styles. Field-dependent people show a repertoire of behaviors which give them access to others when they need information from them as guides to structuring ambiguous situations. The smoother relations with others, facilitated by avoidance of direct expressions of hostility, seem likely to insure continuation of that access. Field-independent people, whose cognitive styles involve greater reliance upon internal referents, have less need for behaviors of this kind and seem less likely to develop them.

✪   ✪   ✪   ✪   ✪

Adaptation to the Cognitive Style of Another

Thus far we have examined attunement between people's cognitive styles and their life circumstances and between an individual's cognitive style and other domains of his behavior. We now turn to still another kind of attunement, this time implicating the reactions of others towards people with different cognitive styles. There is evidence that in social interaction with field-dependent and field-independent people, others respond to them in ways that are adaptive to the needs these people have as a function of their cognitive styles. Specifically, the need field-dependent people have for guidance in structuring situations is recognized by others who behave towards them in ways that will help them achieve structure. Conversely, the ability of field-independent people to function autonomously leads others to allow this autonomy to find expression. Let me give some illustrations.

In a study we did of patient-therapist interactions early in therapy, each therapist was assigned a field-dependent and a field-independent patient. We noticed that, in average word count, the utterances of field-independent patients were about four times as long as the utterances of field-dependent patients. Analyses of the patient-therapist dialogues showed that this difference was a direct consequence of a difference in the structure of the questions the therapists put to each of their two kinds of patients. Each therapist asked more open-ended questions of his field-independent patient and more questions specific enough to be answered "yes" or "no" of his field-dependent patient. The difference in the type of question asked makes understandable the otherwise paradoxical additional result that there were significantly more "no" responses to the therapists' proposals among field-dependent than among the field-independent patients. Obviously, questions that can be answered "yes" or "no" —for example, "Is your father alive?"—have a greater probability of producing "no" responses than questions which are open-ended—for example, "Would you tell me about your family?"

It is not difficult to see that each type of question suits the cognitive style of the patient of whom it is asked. Addressing questions which allow specific responses to field-dependent patients relieves them of the burden of structuring their replies, a competence in which they are limited. In effect, through the form of the question he asks, the therapist assumes responsibility for helping such patients compose a picture, for communication to him, of what they are like and what is bothering them, the primary mission in the very early sessions of therapy. Conversely, with the open-ended questions more commonly addressed to field-independent patients, the task of structuring falls more to the patient. This is a task field-independent patients are better equipped to undertake.

Although this study did not examine the outcome of treatment, it is not difficult to imagine that when the therapist phrases his questions to suit the patient's needs, relations are likely to proceed smoothly between patient and therapist to the probable advantage of the therapeutic outcome. In contrast, were the therapist to persist in asking open-ended questions of his field-dependent patient, the patient would very likely feel uncomfortable with the therapy and unhappy with the therapist. A similar negative outcome would result if highly specific questions were asked of field-independent patients in the face of their preference for structuring situations on their own.

Further evidence that people's cognitive styles influence others' behavior towards them, in ways that are adaptive to their styles, is provided by studies of the treatment modality chosen by therapists for their field-dependent and field-independent patients. Therapists are likely to favor supportive therapy for field-dependent patients and modifying therapy for field-independent patients. In supportive therapy, the therapist assumes considerable responsibility for structuring the form and content of the session. This approach seems suited to the needs of the field-dependent patient. In modifying therapy, patient and therapist roles are given less definition and the patient plays a large part in shaping events. That approach seems suited to the needs of field-independent patients. The choice of one form of treatment or the other in effect signifies a decision on the therapist's part to enter into quite different kinds of social interaction with his patient—an interaction in which the patient's opportunity for structuring the situation is limited or one in which the patient is given more leeway in structuring.

In these studies of which kind of patient is assigned to which kind of therapy, the therapists made the choice of treatment modality for the patient in the initial intake interview. The shift in therapists' question structure I described a moment ago also took place in the very first session of therapy. It appears that "adaptation to the style of another" can occur very rapidly, even in the interaction between people encountering each other for the first time. That a person's cognitive style can quickly have such important and discernible effects on another's behavior towards him suggests that the characteristics involved in the field-dependent and field-independent cognitive styles are highly salient in every day life.

✳ ✳ ✳ ✳ ✳

Mobility and Fixity in the Use of Cognitive Styles

I turn now to a final way in which cognitive styles may figure in personal adaptation. We will be concerned here with the possibility of diversifying the attributes of cognitive styles available to the individual so as to enhance the usefulness of cognitive styles in the service of adjustment.

The cluster of cognitive restructuring skills, and the cluster of interpersonal competencies, as we have seen, have their high and low levels at opposite ends of the field-dependent-independent cognitive-style dimension. While the tendencies for people to be high in one cluster and low in the other are patterns commonly found, there is no reason to believe that these are the only ones possible, or that, once established, they are irretrievably set. It may indeed be possible to acquire access to the characteristics associated with each of the contrasting cognitive styles. In principle, we may expect to find quite often people who, with a good degree of regularity, show the particular cognitive and social characteristics in which a field-dependent style expresses itself, or the particular cognitive and social characteristics in which a field-independent style expresses itself. We may expect to find other people who show the characteristics associated with both styles—in other words, who have cognitive restructuring skills and interpersonal competencies. In a recent extension of field-dependence theory to accommodate these possibilities, we have designated the former kinds of people as "fixed," in the sense of having access to the characteristics of one style or the other; and we have designated those who have access to the characteristics associated with both styles as "mobile." To the extent that, as we have emphasized, each style includes characteristics that are adaptive under specified circumstances, the person who is mobile can, in effect, call upon the characteristics that suit the task at hand. I might note that "mobile" and "fixed" are terms proposed by Werner, although our use of them is different in some important ways.

It seems reasonable to assume that the development of mobility may be fostered both by life experiences and by training. With regard to training, the objective is clearly to help the person, as far as possible, to acquire the characteristics found towards both poles of the field-dependence-independence dimension. Although there has as yet been no work concerned directly with training for mobility, there is evidence that training can affect particular components of the hierarchical structure proposed by field-dependence theory. Thus, it is clear that specific cognitive restructuring skills in which field independence manifests itself can be improved by appropriate educational measures. There is some suggestion as well that training in restructuring as a general competence may result in enhancement of performance on particular restructuring dimensions. And there is also some indication that training people to place greater reliance on bodily referents in perception of the upright may improve performance in such restructuring tasks as disembedding. If generalizability of training effects from one level to another in the hierarchical field-dependence model is established in further research, important conceptual and practical implications would follow. On the conceptual side, evidence of generalizability would demonstrate that the constructs constituting the model are interrelated in ways postulated by field-dependence theory. On the practical side, evidence of generalizability would suggest that educational programs can be devised in which the training given would transfer to functions related to, but not specifically represented in, the program itself. We ourselves are now working on the development of a program of training in cognitive restructuring skills to determine whether it will enhance performance in the whole range of functions conceived to involve restructuring, such as disembedding, closure speed, perspectivism, and so on. This effort to influence developmental changes experimentally complements our earlier approach of studying naturally occurring developmental changes.

Training efforts thus far have been invested in the cognitive-restructuring aspects of field independence only. Training in the interpersonal competencies in which field dependence expresses itself should be an equally plausible enterprise. There is cause for optimism on this point in the finding I noted earlier that the poorer performance of field-independent people in learning social material is a result of their lack of attention to such material rather than a lack of ability to learn it. Inattentiveness should not be difficult to remedy. Also encouraging to the prospects of training in interpersonal competencies are the indications that group encounter programs now in vogue seem able to enhance social sensitivity and effectiveness in interpersonal relations, although the evidence thus far is more impressionistic than systematic.

While much more work is clearly needed, the indications that training in the various components of field dependence-independence is feasible and that training effects may show generalization make development of mobility through appropriate educational programs a hopeful prospect. Mobility, by enlarging the repertoire of adaptive responses available to the individual, gives him the best of both worlds.

Three

Individuality and Diversity

I want to conclude by putting into perspective the conception of individual diversity inherent in a cognitive-style approach. I feel it important to do so because, in order to fit what I have needed to say about cognitive styles and their role in adaptation into the limited time available, I have given less attention than I would have liked to the broader theoretical framework and to the larger research objectives of which the work on cognitive styles has been an integral part.

As noted earlier, the empirical and theoretical work my colleagues and I have done has had as its ultimate concern a better understanding of the structure of personality, in the broadest sense, and of personality development. At the same time, we have tried throughout to keep an eye on the individual. The cognitive-style part of our work has been one component—a major one, of course—of our conception of personal functioning. At no time have we had it as our purpose simply to devise schemes for classifying people. Yet, because cognitive styles are concerned with diversity among people, they fall in the tradition of psychology's long-standing interest in individual differences, and therefore have to be considered among the more recent manifestations of that interest. They are, however, different in important ways from past manifestations. It is only necessary to mention some of these earlier manifestations to see how great the difference is.

As far back as the close of the last century there were psychologists who were concerned with individual differences in perception, including time perception, apprehension of pitch, and pain sensitivity, to cite just a few examples. Soon after, considerable interest developed in individual differences in intellectual characteristics, usually assessed by psychometric means. In both lines of work, the underlying concern was with practical implications of the individual differences observed—for example, in the schools. Another kind of interest in individual differences, which had its heyday at a later time, although actually tracing its origins to antiquity, was expressed in the work on traits and types. More recently, factor analysis has been used to identify individual differences of varying scope.

It is not difficult to identify some of the ways in which these approaches to individual differences are different from the cognitive-style approach. First, however much the earlier approaches vary among themselves, the individual differences they concerned themselves with were characteristically handled at a descriptive level and not rooted in theory. In addition, the variables attended to were usually rather circumscribed. Moreover, the variables were most often of a content rather than a process nature; accordingly, the focus was on the "how much" rather than on the "how" of behavior. Finally, in most instances, the role of contextual factors in the expression of individual differences received only limited attention. Cognitive styles stand apart from most of the earlier approaches in the scope of what they encompass of behavior in the person, in their conceptual underpinning, in their attention to person-situation interactions, and in the developmental context in which they have been placed. Because of these features, it seems appropriate to say that cognitive styles are really concerned with individuality and with diversity among people rather than with individual differences in the usual narrow sense.

In fact, it is this view of cognitive styles which makes it possible for me to believe in their reality, and, at the same time, to find myself altogether comfortable with Kierkegaard's well-known dictum: "Every man is an exception." Let me suggest some of the ways in which grouping people according to cognitive style may yet leave room for the considerable diversity that makes each human being unique.

First, at any level of psychological differentiation, of which the field-dependent and field-independent cognitive styles are expressions, there are to be found a variety of modes of integration. For example, reflecting differences in integration, one relatively field-independent person may be mentally ill, to a point where he requires institutionalization; another may be mentally robust and functioning well at home and in the community. The psychological pictures of these two people of similar cognitive style are of course very different.

Second, the field-dependent and field-independent cognitive styles are process variables, reflecting different structural arrangements in the psyche. Similar structural arrangements, leading to similar modes of information processing, may yet produce great variety in content. For instance, though two relatively field-dependent people may place considerable emphasis on external social referents in forming their attitudes under ambiguous conditions, the specific attitudes at which they arrive may be quite different, depending on a host of factors in their histories and in the immediate situation.

An experience from our research illustrates the possibility that a great variety in content may emanate from the same underlying structures and processes. In a longitudinal study, we obtained figure drawings from the same subjects when they were 10 years old and again when they were 24. These drawings were rated for articulation of body concept, which we take as one indicator of specialization of psychological functions, reflecting developed differentiation. Ratings of the 10- and 24-year drawings, made blindly by the same judge at different times, were found to correlate .78. Later, the judge was told that the two sets of drawings had been made by the same subjects and asked to match them. Although the test-retest correlation was very high, the judge's matches were successful in only about a third of the cases. These two results are not contradictory. The scheme devised to assess drawings for articulation takes account of the "architecture" of the human figure as represented on paper, including, for example, realism in proportioning and in interrelating parts of the body. The very high test-retest correlation indicates that those who portrayed the body in an articulated fashion at age 10, relative to their peer group, were also very likely to do so at age 24. At the same time, content features of the drawings—for example, indicators of sexual awareness, signs of anxiety, and presence or absence of social appurtenances—changed considerably in each subject's drawings from one age to the other. It is obviously the specific content features of a drawing rather than its architecture—its flesh, rather than its skeletal structure—which is mainly responsible for the immediate impression they give to a viewer. Because of this, it is possible to have poor matching in the face of considerable structural similarity. In this particular instance, with similar formal properties of the body concept, there was yet enormous variety in content characteristics.

A third way in which similarity in cognitive style leaves room for diversity lies in the influence of contextual factors on the behavioral sequelae of cognitive styles. I have by now given numerous examples of how particular situational variables may determine the concrete behaviors emanating from the use of a given cognitive style. In fact, I was able to cite instances where opposite behaviors occurred with change in context, although these opposite behaviors were guided by the same underlying stylistic tendency. Certainly, in their manifold expressions, cognitive styles are not in the nature of a soda fountain where turning on a particular spout always causes the same product to come spilling out.

Fourth, and finally, mobility in the use of cognitive styles opens still another route to diversity. The person who acquires access to the characteristics of both a field-dependent and a field-independent cognitive style, and uses each as it suits the situation at hand, is likely to show considerable variety in behavior.

These then are some of the grounds for expecting that people with the particular similarities in their underlying psychological structure responsible for their cognitive styles, and hence in their characteristic mode of processing information, may yet present a great variety of psychological faces. In all these ways, allowance is made for the uniqueness of the individual, which Kierkegaard's dictum implies.

I began the long journey on which I have taken you with a statement of what cognitive styles are. I emphasized particularly that they are pervasive dimensions of individual functioning which cut across the compartments into which man's psychological life has traditionally been divided. Perhaps this holistic view of cognitive styles may have come across to you in a more convincing way as I went on to tell you about the inordinately wide range of psychological phenomena meaningfully implicated in the field-dependent and field-independent cognitive styles. Reflecting their scope, cognitive styles have required a correspondingly broad theoretical framework in which to make themselves at home. The theory proposed for this purpose, however incomplete its propositions and however much in need of further empirical support, seems to have the potential for dealing with the wide range of psychological phenomena involved in cognitive styles, as well as with their causes and consequences. The development of theories which can bring together diverse and previously separate domains within a cohesive conceptual framework is indeed a major goal of psychology as a science.

REFERENCES

Berry, J. W., 1976. *Human ecology and cognitive style: Comparative studies in cultural and psychological adaptation.* New York: John Wiley & Sons.

Bruner, J. S. and D. Krech, eds., 1950. *Perception and personality.* Durham, N.C.: Duke University Press.

Pelto, P. J., 1968. The difference between "tight" and "loose" societies. *Trans-Action* 5, pp. 37-40.

Werner, H., 1957. The concept of development from a comparative and organismic point of view. In D. B. Harris, ed., *The concept of development: An issue in the study of human behavior.* Minneapolis: University of Minnesota Press, pp. 125-148.

Werner, H., 1962. The significance of general experimental psychology for the understanding of abnormal behavior and its correction or prevention. In T. Dembo, and G. Leviton, eds., *The relationship between rehabilitation and psychology. A Conference held at the Institute of Human Development, Clark University, 1959.* Washington, D.C.: Department of Health, Education, and Welfare, Office of Vocational Rehabilitation, pp. 62-74.

Witkin, H. A. and J. W. Berry, 1975. Psychological differentiation in cross-cultural perspective. *Journal of Cross-Cultural Psychology,* 6, pp. 4-87.

Witkin, H. A., P. W. Cox, and F. Friedman, 1976. *Supplement No. 2: Field-dependence-independence and psychological differentiation. Bibliography with index.* Princeton, N.J.: Educational Testing Service (ETS RB 76-28).

Witkin, H. A., P. W. Cox, F. Friedman, A. G. Hrishikesan, and K. N. Siegel, 1974. *Supplement No. 1: Field-dependence-independence and psychological differentiation. Bibliography with index.* Princeton, N.J.: Educational Testing Service (ETS RB 74-42).

Witkin, H. A., R. B. Dyk, H. F. Faterson, D. R. Goodenough, and S. A. Karp, 1974. *Psychological differentiation.* Potomac, Md.: Erlbaum. Orginally published, Wiley, 1962.

Witkin, H. A. and D. R. Goodenough, 1976. *Field-dependence revisited.* Princeton, N.J.: Educational Testing Service (ETS RB 76-39).

Witkin, H. A. and D. R. Goodenough, 1977. Field-dependence and interpersonal behavior. *Psychological Bulletin,* 84, pp. 661-689.

Witkin, H. A., C. A. Moore, D. R. Goodenough, and P. W. Cox, 1977. Field-dependent and field-independent cognitive styles and their educational implications. *Review of Educational Research*, 47, pp. 1-64.

Witkin, H. A., P. K. Oltman, P. W. Cox, E. Ehrlichman, R. M. Hamm, and R. W. Ringler, 1973. *Field-dependence-independence and psychological differentiation: A bibliography through 1972 with index*. Princeton, N.J.: Educational Testing Service (ETS RB 73-62).